# CLOUDS AND RED EARTH

# CLOUDS

## AND

## RED

## EARTH

# Gene Frumkin

Swallow Press  Ohio University Press
Chicago   Athens, Ohio   London

A number of these poems first appeared in the following publications:

A, Café Solo, Chicago Review, Contact II, Crazy Horse, Dacotah Territory, Invisible City, Kayak, Lemming, The Nation, New America, New Mexico Magazine, New Orleans Review, The Only Journal of the Tibetan Kite Society, Oriental Blue Streak, Poetry, Poetry*Texas, Puerto del Sol, Quetzal, Road Apple Review, Southwest Women's Poetry Exchange, Stooge, Turquoise Land, Word, Yankee.

In addition, some of the poems included in this text appeared in The Rainbow-Walker, published by the Grasshopper Press, Albuquerque, Patrick Bolles, publisher.

Swallow Press Books
are published by
The Ohio University Press
Athens, Ohio

Library of Congress Cataloging in Publication Data

Frumkin, Gene.
    Clouds and red earth.

    I. Title.
PS3556.R8C5      811'.54      81-9542
ISBN 0-8040-0418-8         AACR2
ISBN 0-8040-0375-0 (pbk.)

*for* JOHN LOGAN

# CONTENTS

# I PLACEMENTS

# SOULFEATHERS FOR ALBERT CAMUS

In Albuquerque "the relentless
bad taste
          reaches a point of baroque extravagance
where all can be forgiven"
                              The miles
of neon lights along Central Avenue
attract me as no other lights anywhere
I'm a tourist
          nothing more
of this nightly bawdy passage
through the New Mexico plains

Albuquerque is a desert
                         During the day
I can be alone with it    I can make love
to it    How can it resist me
helpless as it is    a city of little character
and no repute?    All it asks of me
is that I bring back flowery stories
from Sante Fe
          60 miles away
Santa Fe is a bitch    We would quarrel incessantly
There would be questions of fidelity

# RELATIONSHIPS

When you say the clouds
are your special friends it is not
to disown the desert sun
this most luminous enchanter
for whom you bear your life
in a suitcase
                    The clouds are
a respite and a seclusion
You converse with them alone
at a table in the dingy smokehole
of a bar    The clouds inhabit
a can of Coors as easily as
any other space
                    When you
lug yourself along under the sun,
that crisp sun so high a swinger
in New Mexico, there is always something
you leave behind    a forgotten
story    a wise caution
You neglect yourself    as if you were
a strip of celluloid
                    When the clouds
come around you can tell them this
they know what you mean

# BANDELIER FOREST

Fir and pine
as they delineate the heights
recast the quality of light
These trees hold
within their branches
a sudden weight
which is of the eye

Still summer
and the sun is a gathering
of remembrances
its light a deer or dog
clinging to the scent everywhere
along the curving road

On either side the tall
fir and pine
the aspen    massive
tree-laden light
The eye drives directly
into the slow, measured walls
streaming down
and is absorbed in shadows
in shadows of windows

# TALL COUNTRY

It was a while before the woods
    showed up, while the cloudmasks overhead
        shimmered, greyish blood
  The hawk now spreads
his wings—his claws clasp wires
    along invisibly winding trails—
        holds fast to the wiles
  of air, and flares repeatedly into black spires

All birds are below the high fir
    Lower still, regions of human craft
        spoken in the loft
  of smoke, small tumors of desire
that grow upward with toxic grace
    though never so high as these trees
        where mountain goats graze
  never too near the gods who mute this place

Now the weather shifts toward elegance
    (an English garden, yellow roses
        lilies and lilacs, trim praises
  of hedge and cypress), intelligence
absorbed in stealth by woods and hawks
    The gods commence to speak
        translucent arrows of a book:
  to be read quickly in the glance of rocks

in a gust of pine, in faces that hide
    behind blue shade, nothing seen
        but what is in the sun
  nothing heard but what's inside
the cave of tongues    So it is, the field
    tall country displays
        to eyes that inwardly gaze
  Breath sucks in whatever gods have failed

# SUMMER STORM, ALBUQUERQUE

How to come near
so near your breath relives
another's death
           You hear
the cicadas' electric circuits
that unison of many lives
tuned
      to one purpose
               Sweat
pours from the nerves
unseen
       consumed by breathing
in quick beats   the woman
clammed up in her skin
by your wasteful humidity
                 She is
unable to speak not knowing who
she is   that you have stolen
across her life
in grey gasps   that you hide
her light in your glowering head
the grey
        hair the brain
covering the hot summer
glow in her groin
            the rain
beating down in rivers
              pods
breaking open
           bursting phlegm
of the gods releasing you at last
until in half an hour
you are quiet

            stilled by the tranquil
capsule of an emergent sun
your heart blue again in
its usual space
                The secret of who
she was
          not disclosed    you are still
a ghost in whom she did not
believe
         It is warm and moist
afterwards    the thunder with which
you pleaded for her mouth
was only your hard, heaving breath
and was not heard

# DRIVING TO CUBA, NEW MEXICO

*for* WILLIAM EASTLAKE

Mesas in the distance
lavender
      the cliffs layer on layer
russet green and beige
Two hours being driven
          half dozing in
such calm no cage could hold
seeing the sun roam four-footed
across the plain
        The land sprang toward the
honeyed giant
        through the grey campfire
of my sleep
     Beauty
        what does it mean
but the beast arrested mid-leap
between morning and night
          to be clothed always
in the moment's scent
       We came
to the ranch    I climbed its mesa
as if to verify this permanence
this brief blossoming in the ages' span
And found in fossilized wood
a landscape by Cezanne

# MADRID PHOTOGRAPH

*for* JILL


There is a girl who hitchhikes
from one month to the next    camps in
damp woods talks to the moths that
hover over blue campfires    Her word is
Today Today    as if no time could atone
for a lost father as if the burning owls
on their branches would expire if no eyes
answered    The pieces of her life
are water the Pacific saltspray raw solace
for the smooth stone behind the forehead
of each day    It is the clock in the talk
of men she runs from

                              I saw a photograph
Madrid New Mexico 1969    hair
over shoulders reconciled to the length
of a near-deserted mining town    her eyes
had traveled centuries    a face inhabited by
slow summer at the beginning of autumn
the leaves to be taken home
and pasted on fresh windows    Her face gazed
into the laurel of the lens    a wisp
in the communion of all joys and sorrows

And where shall she go    by what process
the calculus of love be recognized and how
dare she devise a reckoning?    I told her
a dream I had    in which he (who was not
named) floated within the curving air while
the room stared    floated until I who have
heard the secrets of birds (without understanding)
welcomed him back, confetti fluttering
in my head    His face no more than

a thumbprint in my eyes I asked
"How do you do it?"   He said "It's easy
Just let go of the ground"   And I released
my feet from earth and rose in a current
of light almost to the ceiling

                        There is a girl
who must create the man possessed of such
hardly human skill   who holds the wild bouquet
to ease him down and radical numbers to bind his
heaven and earth together

# AT THE D.H. LAWRENCE COTTAGE

Chopping wood with a dry axe
3 blisters in 20 minutes    rhythm at
half strength    4 chunks and a tall Coors
2 cheers for Lawrence comrados
& his antique typewriter in San Cristobal
          one for the bull on his cottage
the other for that phoenix
painted on his pine
                              the third cheer
absent / he's an old
wide-brimmed hat a blue shirt
he's a suitcase

There were friends and guests
who talked and drank    Lawrence's ghost
hiding below with mice    holding out
for the dark
              the dark man
a fiction
              The British prof and I
strolled to see the summer's Fellow
Coffee and a cigar
Frieda unmentioned in the talk
          Lawrence invisible
   Come out
                    come out
     take off your dust jacket
let the horses nibble
at your beard

# THE COLORS OF TIME

*for* JOHN LOGAN

There's barely time

    Original wood
    framework to hold infiltration of silica
    and secondary deposits / iron oxides
    in small quantities

      Agatized rainbows

    Hollows in the wood hold
    crystals of quartz harder than steel

    166 lbs per cubic foot
        after resurrection

You are a letter away
    By rushing water

        The aspen leaves
        have fallen here

        A Halloween wind drives in
        from the west
            with cosmic rustling of sheets

        Milky Ways
            for the candy-callers

    Transported by Triassic flood waters
    sediments built up
    over 400 feet thick across the plain
    When the Rockies rose

13

from the settled land mass
erosion began / the logs
drifted toward immortality

As the colors of time
knock at my heart
I write these lines for you
an hour from Erie

      Barely time for a
            glass of lavender wood

      All the masks are dying

OUR SHIPS ARE PASSING
      Their bright flags
      snap in the storm

# EL CONQUISTADOR:
## THE SEVENTH FLOOR

*for* STANLEY NOYES

On the seventh floor one 40-watt bulb
stayed awake through the shades of moon and sun
to tint the corridors with coppery light

On the seventh floor we could gaze
back at ourselves    figures in a brown daguerreotype
of some historical dimension
                                        in which we could

observe ourselves staring back like Spanish dons
There was barely enough candlefaith on that level
for us to believe we would some later time

exist
              A university in northern New Mexico
consumed by vacancy on the seventh floor
of its tallest dorm during those spring hours

when gods and sybils are called to leap
from their graves    a university which awkwardly
flickered us on toward the blue light of another

emergence
                Now we see it as ancient film:
the day-nightwatchman maintaining his indignant search
on the seventh floor for two men of words

who slept in one chamber that one night
and still are heard to whisper in the walls
and still conspire there in their coral afterglow

# "GOODBYE, LOVES"

*for* DAVID & MONA JOHNSON


SAN FRANCISCO (UPI)—A 20-year-old hippie, high
on drugs, shouted "Goodbye, Loves" and jumped the
275 feet from the Golden Gate Bridge into San Fran-
cisco Bay with his sandals in his hand Tuesday.

He came up singing from a plunge that has taken
364 lives.


1    Las Truchas

These clouds do not conclude

They are indigo, grey, in portions unwashed
white    yellowish substrata appear
as windows of dried sweat in the sky over
Truchas    It is a late-afternoon hour of
mourning    for what, none of us
can say    Perhaps it is we ourselves
who mourn for those irresolute agencies
moving slowly through our eyes
disguised as clouds

                        As we entered
the town we met a torn building
black from burning    small windows /
skull's eyes    A one-lane main street
thinly layered in asphalt
                        Fernandez
the garage-man told us where
White's gallery was "go down there about 7 blocks
                        the Presbyterian Church
                        a picket fence
                        20 feet high    only one in town"

WHITE'S GALLERY
VISITORS
WELCOME

This town was *Toledo*    horizontal and
brown adobe    It was
Spain
        brown vision of Spain
the penitent eyes    under the marshals
of heaven, hoary, holding splintered batons
"electrified" (as today's tongue
consumes the spiritual field off
in the distance
                O specters
children smiling
                your teeth small white clocks
that themselves don't know
what time it is

            2   Lama

They welcomed us to Lama with
communal smiles    (This place a domestic
physical moon    men bearded    women
in long skirts)
            and offered us
home-baked bread spread with goat's cheese
alfalfa sprouts
            An ex-Marine corporal
Eric
      filing a curved chunk of branch
gripped in a vise explained
the 5:30 a.m. bell for voluntary meditation

the bell at 6:30 for imperative planning
breakfast and to work at 8
                              building
the women cooking 3 meals a day for 30
in evening dancing & chanting
                              the ashram
not yet structured the dues not yet
regulated hours of labor to equal 7
which could equal 6 or 5 as to
one's ability    not to be codified

Paraphrase:
                "Physical dominant over spiritual now
                as to our nascent need"

The brochure:
                "It should be understood that
                Lama Foundation provides only
                the rudiments—tools and working area
                What the individual makes of them
                will depend on
                              the sort of energy
                he is willing to commit
                to this effort    We emphasize
                the extraordinary difficulties
                involved on all levels
                              of this work"

Eric
        blond muscular    eyes voyaging
toward the earthly moon    shaping a twisted
bit of branch into something    whatever
humanly necessary    The black girl said
"He's beautiful used to be
                        in the Marines has
the discipline"

Part of a play written /
the labor in his hands, gloved
smoothing down the wood

"We realize that for something new
to be born
something old
must die"

Those who would live on this
moon above Taos
should speak to themselves
honestly

3   Las Truchas

Sunlight at 9000 feet unimpeded strikes through
to the vein streams down the mountains
of the brain across the brow
into prophetic sight    white shadow
is monolithically black no light refracted
intense opposition to prisms
which comprise the heart    in one day
we met Manicheus face to ass

The Trouts is airless Lama perhaps
all air
White's gallery was an open
crypt the body punished to salvage it
for Jesus' mercy    self-taught paintings
had learned the ropes and whips, the chains
that thrash and lead a man to his personal
Calvary    union in pain with One
Who spared Himself none
White himself
no angel in the Body of Christ but an Anglo

detached enough to bear a lantern
into the coffin where the town's Penitentes
prayed as he listened to the Spanish cantor
chant the *albados* in praise
of the Holy Sacraments    singing in his gut
the same stanzas White long white hair
near his heart the six-shooter    silver bullets
scattered throughout his head

St. John of the Cross:

> I live without inhabiting
> Myself—in such wise that I
> Am dying that I do not die

The morada "is easy to identify because
it is usually long and low close to
the earth    Its length usually several times
its width shaped not unlike a coffin
Its massive walls are of hand-textured adobe
giving the structure a unique organic
sculptured quality    It is the essence
of simplicity in design"

Truchas confined to an old fever dozes
through its days
                    (these clouds
do not conclude)
                    at night in heat
squirms and turns on its cliffside
torturing itself to
        in one violent motion
                            in one last straining
ecstasy
        drop from the Sangre de Cristos
to the dead far down

"Their dead march with them
in the Paschal season    They require no Easter
The Resurrection is present in their tapers
their flutes clackers matracas and
occasionally a drum"

4    Lama

Whom to believe?
                    The head lightens
and is held in a leaf    Earth swells
in its pod
                10 lbs of peas
at this height
                Lama
onions alfalfa lima beans    water trickling
into the gulley steadily
                        and the head
enters a green album    arranged
pictures of love torn from the wilderness
and we look
                into the eyes of a goat

Out of the sullen streets of individual
existence rises the dome of assertion
To the solar eminence these people address
their letters and craft    They ask of You
warmth Your flowering radiance
aware that You are purely there insentient
a keg of fire    bodiless unagonized
We pour Your golden blood into our spirits
get drunk on sheer light
                        And Christ
is a dead man whose presence here
consumes the pagan passion    rites

21

of soil tribal paternity worship of
the clouds
                    that do not conclude

Those who depart, to California or
India, shall return
                    Who are the dead
but ourselves?
                    Observe a radish
dip a finger into mud
sit on a log    You have achieved
life and henceforth walk among
the godstruck    Hard on this hillside
they hollow wholeness out of absence
Calm is king in the hushed claims
of holiness
                    Rapture is death
Those who drink goat's milk
are bones in the meadow of Krishna

If they hold to their course
there is an Orpheus for everyone

              5    Las Truchas

Finally to arrange these distortions
if they are    Your years of crime
pour through your bandages    There are pools
of lilac and oregano behind your grimy
lids changing form as the blood charges
through its circuits as the nerves
close in upon the horses prancing in the lamplit
streets    It is night in the tabernacle
where the years' catch of wounded lie
Poor fish they are! fetid and rotten
Who could eat them

                    or lick
such wounds
                    Arthritis has whipped
Mr. White into a hump a hunch
Art has fattened him (his primitive guess
at the poison in his bones buried in the mounds
under the prison of his
brain)    And he said:

          They bury their dead in the ground
          of their church    and when the dead
          grow too numerous they stuff the bones
          into the adobe walls    After many rains
          when the walls have been washed thin
          a thigh or arm reaches through
          projects into air    (again the air)
          groping for air    So many bones stick out
          so many pegs a man could climb them
          all the way up to the cross

White says he has died already
he has nothing to fear
                         not even
the Postmaster of Truchas
                         his town's
chief political figure and foe
"I know who stole my files"
"I'm going to paint flowers on my kitchen window"
"Monday I'll go to his house
with my gun"    "The kids raise hell at night"
"It's so peaceful here"    "The smart ones
move away"    "They drive at 90 down the narrow
street drunk bang bang bang"    "I love it
in Truchas"    "If he doesn't return my files
I'll start banging"    "They burned down
the hardware store in the April uprising

Emanuel is too nice"    "The Postmaster controls
the Welfare"    "You have to be ready
to shoot"    "It's a restful town the dead
are beautiful"

Aromas of earth    calm of the
nightworld insects in molecular whirl
ants and roaches at their duty
on pavement  and dirt    Stare at them
sufficiently and you too crawl swiftly
among them one with such lucid striving
while higher the lamps swarm harshly
into dark air    They do not help you
to see / the eyes are trained to motions
beyond light the heart waits in shadows
it waits for a garden to bloom
out of song as the song enters the Savior's
pierced flesh and the Mother of Sorrows
embraces Him ah! Their gloomy love
You stand holding your breath in
your fingertips the rain runs down
your cheeks all you remember
is the island where you were young
the fruit on the trees the sap glued
to the bark    You begin to walk
and walk until the dog announces himself
turn back drenched by the years
bitten by teeth that surprise you
from a distance    Do you Believe?
In nothing but sun and moon
in what they have accomplished by their incessant
turning as you have stood
alone in the night
accepting your own presence fully at last

a youth again    The lady with golden hair
who emerges from the doorway
is surely a goddess

### 6    Lama

*Tammuz and Ishtar*    the Cult of Life
returns from Christ's agony
formed as a child who eats
the goatcheese
                    of the new moon

  "Where the grass was not, the grass is eaten,
    Where water was not, water is drunk,
    Where the cattle sheds were not, cattle sheds are built"

The clouds do not conclude
but open heaven again for the pagan
goddess the youth's mother his sister
his lover

                    Christ the fallen King
dies forever the church is fallow
His embassy closed    We cannot relive Him
with our suffering    He will refuse to sip our blood
at our last supper preferring as always
a fried catfish
                    The dead merely stretch their arms
outward from the earth's moon and grasp
the rains of spring to serve our eyes
that survey so curiously the surface of things
The dead have been here before
and lead us into that memory through which
we must newly pass

Deliver us
Adonis from the darkness of Hades
Gentle youth    long brown hair brown eyes
beloved of Aphrodite    wounded early
dead too soon    O Lazarus in maroon doublet
and cardinal leotards healed
it must abstractly be said
                                        by beauty
that whispering song of our bones
How lovingly we fuck with nature
when Adonis ploughs the seed of our phallus
and Aphrodite harvests the swollen grain


I structure our most ancient epic into
personal terms
                            Handsome and profound source
first prince of my annals:
my own son almost 7    My daughter
somewhat older and cooler
                                        oracle
of my only temple
                            There is a man
there is a woman
                            a child is born
No faith outlives the order
of this procedure
                            Then quickly
while the wind holds me in the cup
of my singing fall    as I pretend to be
Icarus tripping headlong toward the wise
embrace of the sea I flap my sandals
flap flap
                in air
                            my long hair
pulls me back skyward I'm in the middle

of a marriage I'm the center
of incomparable solace I originate
and I conclude
                    I    ee    why    ee        eye am
swimming among fishes ready
to rise again to the surface
                              to humor every crisis

That is the lyric that issues me
firefly wings the shiny
beetle coat   "America the Beautiful" the flying
hippie sang, after death   Of course of course
another strophe another stroke

# II PROPORTIONS

# PLACITAS NIGHT

*for* STEVE, ROI & NEIL


How    as you walk from
      this moon
that casts a shadowy oval
 on the cloudlit sky
leaving the car stuck in earth
    as you cower
      under the moon
you are one candle
among stones
 a sputtering on two feet

There is no word

Behind / retreating from
 a silverless mine    home for
 snakes gophers moles of the ages

You are heading toward

The way you came down
has not held its ground    It has
not waited
    The moon
holds you to its chart
 Holds
    you run
      Soon

It comes    in this lost plot
a nowhere

the gathering up of all
comings & goings
You are together at last
with yourself   The wings in your gut
strain at the walls   they can't get out
they'll never
                    Slow    slowly
you know
                    that the moon
has entered your life    You go on

# THE SLIT THE BLUE

Behind your eyelids
the planet carries its load of blueberries
horses plunge one by one into dark arroyos
Lenny Bruce sings the Star-Spangled Banner
a black dragon spits blood

You try to stop its turning
for an instant hold it still    catch one thing
purely in your mind
The soap says ENJOY LIFE

A woman pauses before the camera
and speaks    Is that what you heard
that golden rain as it struck the sidewalk
become cellophane    an orange
rolling into the gutter    She stoops
one arm straight down
reaches for it
                    Her flowered parasol
lifts her toward the hawk that hovers
hovers    for you also?

Then it happens    an opening
a slit a blue
                    What had called to you
is your answer    You are among the stars
chained to nothing but your senses
Death is your neighbor    someday he will
borrow you    But so far from your marble planet
you have forgotten what earlier
was broken glass in your fist

When you return    there your body stands
with its fireplace and slippers    Again the barrier
of eyelids   the countryside to be irrigated
day in and out   the horses fed
the dragon locked again into the night

O not the same now    no more    never
The stars travel with you    all space
enters your lungs when you breathe
Woman rain orange might have been other metaphors
What is unalterable
                              the slit the blue
Your former self follows you    a grey shade
in a cloudless afternoon

# WINTER PASSAGE

For weeks the sun
cold
     To itself
             another
Not the source    There
only as white is on the snow

     Your body
wrapped in its coat
has left Grapes of Wrath New York on a
northerly route for Naked Lunch India

Driving    snow mountains
distant on your windshield    Closer
the red clay    indigo clefts
in the Sandias, rosy
snowrugs along the road    sunfrost
     over the land

     As you go deeper
deeper you go home / New York
City where your body
stumbled from its cave

     Home / your skin
as it absorbs the road
warmed by these mountains

     "The way a
person holds his
body
     and moves it"

New York / 1935
playing bottle caps
before the synagogue
little boy's body
shivering under God

You arrive
        and your body
arrives
        at the same
                historic marker:

in Santa Fe you buy
a black Navajo hat with flat rim
feather stuck in the high
dome's band    Stand
in the Plaza    black coat hooked
to the neck
Everybody looks / you dance
war whooping
    around the bandstand
        Such dark and quirky
drag
        Charms for the new Chief
Rabbi of Albuquerque

# THE CORAL FISH

*for* ROBERT BLY

> It was shortly afterwards, when I was making a field
> study of coral fish in warm seas, among which the
> function of aggression in the preservation of the species
> is plain, that the impulse to write this book came to
> me.
> —Konrad Lorenz, *On Aggression*


Demoiselles hiding in the hand's caves
swim forth to drive away
                                    the enemy
        their replicas
                        themselves?
That blue trigger you hold
must finally kill the picassofish
No rival heaven may darken
the starry sky's
                        Your hand
so much alone
                contains living water
seeping and receding
                        through the skin's skull's eyes
(crust on crust
                        whatever area
you've ever occupied)
                        Your hand
in act    gives back to time
those floral formations you have
by breath and sorrow
ingested    (when night descends
the beau gregorys

                    are dreams / flamboyant fires
locked in grey files)    surfacing
a crude sensual force
                    that submerged
rages against itself


                This is
the purport
                Swarms    swarms
lovely small swimmers    salty bodies
flow from sleep into creation
as your hand steps lightly from
the sea's bedding of kelp
into the air
            so fair
                    soaked in apples

# SUPPER AT O'HENRY'S COUNTRY BAR-B-QUE

"They shot the lights out" Frycook says
Last night's brawl
                      on High Chaparral or
            mankind?
                        As Ray Charles
weeps hosannas in his box
                          As bombs
blossom in psychedelic rows
on rail- and harbor-towns
men and women of America labor
in Los Alamos Alamagordo Las Vegas and LA
by vectors of egglight
wasting their eyes

Wet glass sticks
to the slick table    simple needs
resist us    We lose our minds
in a foreign tongue our best sperm
eaten by strangers

Drops of water    drops of
grease    love is heating its last raisins
in the bellies of men

and the stars    are falling    like snow
descending as fire on that other land

            As Joan Baez says farewell
to Angelina
            fire also dies
it also dies    when the food runs out    love is
charcoal    what is left afterwards
in black lumps

# THE INTELLECTUALS AT OKIE'S BAR

*for* GUS BLAISDELL

They are lovers of their own distortions
who sit in such darkness    music
steaming about them
                              beer swelling
their muscles / sense and temperance
tortured into hours of speech
to dowse their minds' reflection
                                        Ocean at night
leaps up in tongues of green illuminated
spume    and dies on sand
A residual humor flaps its wings
evacuates into air
                        The bar is
headquarters for difficult gymnastics

There is nothing outside but stars
and a sliced moon    cold now in November that
arrogant Heaven peopled by the dead
Cars wearing holsters cruise
the boulevard
                        at one with those harmonious
seasons and cycles to which
the balls of drunks aspire:
                                        to be contained
in Purpose    molten fluid pouring
through strict cylinders
                                        to arrive at
the laurel bush at last    completely relieved
done with hessian duty    into the arms
of a goddess more woman than ghost

We are not the mob that coils
around Fortune's rim    Snake eyes
inhabit our bones

                    seeing fumes
canopy all gay processions (prophesy also
the pit where brains are buried)
                                    so we refuse
to march
                hippity-hop through Hell instead
our toes quick
                    as red coals
spend our laughter in heads of foam
matching the need for bright occasions

# PEOPLE

People you bastards
who can blame you on the times

It's no one's fault in early June
the poppies have already died

New Mexico is in heat now
wanting to fuck whatever it can

without courtesy or grace
Emerged from their grassy tombs

miller moths annoy the evening lights
Along the Rio Grande mosquitoes

riving heavy air desire
nothing but random flesh

Though the human heart
is hot for warmth

our politician in his white suit
enters a building

madly bent
                on official business

# THE ANGLO COORDINATOR

As the Anglo coordinator
for the 3rd Annual Southwest Poetry Conference
I have so far failed
to coordinate a single Anglo

I am neurotically troubled
The event is a mere two weeks off
in Durango Colorado
and I freak at the vision
of all those uncoordinated Anglos tripping
over their own feet

I have no doubt the Chicanos and Indians
are in talented hands
but my Anglos, what a confused team
I'll have on my conscience!

None of them knows
the signals I have not yet devised
nor the comprehensive strategy to be used
in delivering our poems
True, the element of surprise
will be on our side
but what we critically lack is the totally expected

Can we depend on the others
to fuck up their lines?    No right-minded coordinator
would risk it    It is time for a
hasty ill-conceived locker-room prayer
something like: "Dear Almighty of the Anglos
bless our flabby metrics our dull rhymes
and give us credit for lots of guts"

Our Almighty is known to be half-hearted
much lazier and probably more incompetent than theirs
Still, he may help us put together
a potent stanza in the right place
a quick spurt of highly-regarded images . . .

though I think it's really no use
The 3rd Annual Southwest Poetry Conference in Durango
is sure to be a slaughter
You can imagine how guilty I feel

# FRAY MARCOS DE MENA

History records Fray Marcos de Mena
as the one who told it, one survivor
from the many shipwrecked, waylaid and slain
at the great water. One of three friars

and two sailors who came back to rescue
two Dominican fathers, by then already dead,
upstream. The canoe was still there
where it had been left in flight before.

Fray Marcos and the others paddled
up the river, sighted two small islands,
landed on one to retire for the night.
As it comes to us, this island quickly heaved up

its human burden, threw all of them overboard,
then vanished. Even so slight a portion
of land refused to allow them their sleep—
God's faithful and their men of water.

Frightened by life and by death exhausted,
they thrashed about in the river,
groped about for a solid remnant
of their past, some asylum on *this* shore

of the grave. And another island grew there
in the flow of their death and they arrived,
redeemed another time. From this place,
Fray Marcos tells us, these five Spaniards

saw the other two islands amazingly re-emerge
from the water. In 1553 two whales
swam down the Rio Grande toward the Gulf of Mexico.
Fray Marcos would not lie. Before God

whales were small islands in the Rio Grande.

# BITTER & SWEET

Young women's mouths are sugar
Their spit sweetens the old man's tea
which is bitter

                    bitter the leaves
of coyote-brush and bitter the coreopsis
the mistletoe and thelesperma

                              Sweet
the mouths of young women
who clear their breath with spurge root
who chew fine corn meal to a paste

Bitter the old man's tea
while young women take water
into their mouths to soften still more

the pasty corn    Their spit is sugar
for the old man's tea
He drinks bowl after bowl

bitter with sweet    And though
he does not kiss any young woman's mouth,
he remembers    His tea is hot
                              is hot

# INDIAN CORN

Indian corn suspended from the ceiling
eight ears wired together   One is yellow
one maroon another pink still another black
These colors are imprecise   they harmonize
with, and are, the language that observes them
hanging, at this angle, just above
the horizontal window   This angle
is the eye's
                Another corn is creamy
three others have no words   The numbering
is exact, the sizes of corn descend
from smallest to largest
with two exceptions; again, there is definition
in the numbering
                    These cornshapes have been hanging
around for more than two years, the exact date
of their acquisition lost
though the place, Acoma Pueblo, remains
They instill no ideas
no fantasies   The mind, holding them, is static
itself suspended; the hand has no impulse
to covet their polished surface   What is of concern
is that, at last, they are visible

# BIRTHDAY PARTY AT
## JEMEZ SPRINGS

I sat on that rock
and let the sun melt in my face
There was the stream below
as I had for years imagined it
delicately blue frothing over stones
an 18th century sound
Handel at peace with his heart
It ran to meet the sun
an eighth-mile up    a strip
of gold pulsating    Fireworks
for my daughter's birthday
the girls on their own island midstream
Before that were the horses
five of them, wild    I took their pictures
as they grazed on the other bank
Paul threw stones and laughed
at the small geysers
Lydia tiptoed to the girls' island
and became a blue sweater

With lords & ladies dancing
atop the New Mexico mesas
I thought of Vietnam
and the impossible poem
Those fireworks there! I had never
seen them    What was a child
without skin    Whose mother
lay there in her own green juice
What flowers grew
in Dean Rusk's eyes

Handel in his barge on the Thames
had also heard of war
but wrote music    Horses knew
nothing of war and wrote nothing
My amulets were lost in water
Another stone another splash
A brown wind arose from the north
Girls and mother left
the island    Time to go
Sherry officially 11

My mind is not
bloody enough    I listen for
Handel while the Stones
bless our age for what "could be
the last time"

Lords & ladies I'll believe
any gossip you tell me
Tell me about the
roses and cherry trees
that blossomed in your shires
Let me hear you scream
as your wigs catch fire

# DRINKING IN JUAREZ

### 1    Drinking at the Manhattan Bar

We had squid    sweet with slight salt
at the Alcazar    A whim to be
photographed    The sleep on our faces
deceived the lens    All that drinking
and we were cleverly awake    We could
write our names on the tablecloth
in squid ink
                    All that drinking priorly
slings and zombies    at the Manhattan Bar
two blocks from the bridge in Juarez

and long talk    the sergeant from
Fort Bliss his daddy the ex-jockey
and the sergeant's half brother half Chicano
half American Legion from Korea
"All those people I killed"    a whimper
huge gentle half Chicano    He'd probably killed
no one / Billy Calley inked on his breast
in rum & coke, a dream image
of desired guilt
                    All that drinking
Benny the sergeant raised horses
on a hundred acres in Texas
His daddy once rode horses as he must have
ridden his Chicano woman:  with tight reins
and a loose lip    He was prancing
up and down the long narrow bar    a pint
for his every size    a squirt
for the mod hip chicks next table
All that drinking
                    Benny was serious
"Should have dropped the Bomb
on China in '58    No Vietnam"
We drank and listened like spiders

comrades in nothing that mattered
I said (because it didn't matter) "I'm a Jew"
and Benny loved it that I was a Jew
and taught English at the university
in New Mexico
                              His daughter may show up
in one of my classes soon    That's how much
we loved each other


2    Drinking in the Shangri-La


Our first stop was Shangri-La
after a long drive in the sun
after going wrong in wallowing traffic
going as far off course as the church
solemn Mexicans on the steps
in the plaza the streets    jostling
chanting praying on the anniversary
of Christ's Crucifixion    at 3
in the afternoon Good Friday 1971
and we, the two of us, weary
hungry    unblessed on our difficult way
toward blindness toward some godless
Parnassus of the mind
mountain of no will and no desire
two travelers with our hearts in the air
we drove through the dark shapes
slow as sheep    Christ without us
without Christ we ascended
slowly    our vehicle a light
pagan blue    and got beyond the religious
civilities into more delicate sanctuary
we got there    a policeman directed us
and it was cool inside    Shangri-La,
we found, is not a crowded place
in the middle hours    we felt younger

less tired on the fringe of No Mind
Gin & tonic was our desire
not lamentation nor prophecy
not song nor the heavenly spire
Resurrection was a gin & tonic
that's how it was that good day
when Christ carried his death up Calvary


3    Drinking in the Alcazar


We arrived in Mexico's fourth largest city
followed by America    America flowed
across the bridges from El Paso    America
sat beside us in the Alcazar where we
drank sherry
                    A Mexican tenor
serenaded the four couples    He sang
"O how we danced
                        on the night
      we were wed"
in Spanish    I had a religious impulse
to drink another sherry to toast the bride
or the groom    whichever best represented
the influence of Yiddish comedians
on American culture    I thought of
Barbra Streisand the songs of Jerry Lewis
how American "my people" were
as some perhaps sat there groggy-eyed
remembering how they were married
in a Broadway play
                        We drank more
sherry    the Alcazar's waiters performed
their trick    letting wine from the flask
roar down their gullets from a distance
of twenty Basque feet

                    The Mexican tenor
lost his voice    our neighbors from America
lost their smiles and compliments
I lost my checkbook    or somebody
stole it    later a check for $130.00
turned up in my American bank    "#1063 Reported
Stolen—Signature Irreg."
                    We had
our picture taken ordered another sherry
We were very merry    America was with us
I think it was the Mexican tenor
who flashed our picture as he flew past


        4    Drinking in the Lux


It was beer and tequila
at the Lux    two long nights
as we argued with Dante Alighieri
about the propriety of light
at the bottom of volcanoes    he contending
there was no circle for such light:
a mere moon in a watery eyelid

The children of Juarez are hideous
their eyes are beasts
                    hungry so young
they quiver in the entrails of the tourists
who rarely know they've been so sneakily struck

Beatrice was Rosario the first night
Teresa the second    Rosario drank
orange juice but Teresa drank beer
Rosario was worth $10 but Teresa
only nine    Teresa insulted Gloria
in the middle of Gloria's grinding ass


                    53

Rosario was not there the second night
It was a student Antonio who
introduced us to both    Dante was there
looking for Beatrice too, there at the Lux
He said there was no light in basements
We said in America there existed
flashlights    He hadn't heard of them
but said in basements dark was the proper motive

The children of Juarez sell
American cigarettes to Americans
They are hideous    not to be trusted

Two long nights quickly spent
to our last few dollars    Dante said
he was in exile from the sun
We noted it was night in any case    He said
we were all in exile    We began
to wonder    Teresa said he was a creep in Mexican
We smoked all the cigarettes Steve had bought
from the children of Juarez
Dante said the lighted tip of a cigarette
reminded him of Mount Etna
Old nostalgic divinity student, I thought
Next thing he'll be bawling
in memory of Benito Mussolini

The children of Juarez are minefields
I must remember to step around them
on tiptoe
                If I should touch one
I'd fly apart

All that drinking in the Lux
the dollars spent    This was
the bottom of something    the light
of something    We were dimmed and dowsed
two nights in a row    Only Dante
was clear    As we walked to our hotel
I said "Observe the celestial affluence"
while pointing to the ground
A lady named Beatrice halted
as we passed    "Can't you guys
walk straight?"    "The light of Dante
is blinding us" Steve said    "More likely
it's the dark    Dante is a creep"
said Beatrice    who was in her 40's
accompanied by three male adults

We flew to the Hotel San Antonio
like falling stars
                    that last night
glad the children of Juarez were all asleep

# RAINBOW DOME

My friends have built a rainbow
dome / wood and cartops
 old sinks and toilets
sun for heating

  Earth is cold

One of them a writer
 quit writing
  to bide and bide
"This is too important
 to be wrong about"

  By themselves
bunched together a tribe
"We are different
 from other people"

   Earth is black it's white

They pray to the manycolored
sun Eat from one pocket
to another / many flavors
from emptiness
 sukiyaki redwine eggplant
They will make their own
 carrots and corn
 feed the chickens milk the goat
Some dreams they live
    are acid rainbows
some simply springwater or
red mesas
They say hello every morning
  to the sky
(Too important to
  say it wrong)

They are miles from me
the city cat  who dines on mountains
in my famous alleys

Earth is snow and golden aspen

I stay and stay
too full to move away

# THE BEADS

*for* JUDY GRAHN

Small black birds   kangaroo rat bones
a feather   ringed on a double string
with beads round and long   palette
and rosary   on which to count
minute blessings
                    those we are afraid
to touch   the bubbles in our blood

The woman's gift of beads
crystals your need to
swell up your life
to ride the red engines of calm
higher   past the broken armor
rusting in fields   trees charred
legs and brains floating in water

Your self's other enemies are clouds
that swallow the nearby mountains
saying "You also must lose your self"
They would dispel the beads   "You are
no larger on the starry thread"

Joy is helpless against such wispy
mystics   To protest their vanity
is to risk a gaudy death   They will not
allow you the priest who dances
only for your eyes   They say
"Live toward infinity   become air
Add your soul to the eternal numbering"

Ah, your new beads clothe you
in a spell    Small black birds
kangaroo rat bones    a feather    This is
whitest witchcraft    Your body escapes
its bottle and is of an element
with Earth
                You count the blessings
giant-colors in the hand

# FLOATING

It is this, finally, with woven insight
to arrange the terms in such balance
all wavering is canceled    Seaward drifts
the captain and homeward the fragrances
There is daybreak to reconcile
with a short goodbye
                              I have seen
the iris blossom and quickly die
Pigments maps elegies stored
for 40 years    alone I lie there
weaving madras stripes in air
Am I the captain or the sea


No answer but to rise when the
phone rings    and say "Hello
Come on over"    as my body floats
across the month of May
                              over the Rockies
a painted Indian a painful rug
floats floats
                   while someone rushes to me
bringing a heavy notebook
                              a body

# LANDSCAPE IN GREY

Fields and mountains grey
as the first winter cloudlight
sets across the land
The road is grey
the deer grey cattle grey
no sun no moon
Shelter from all other colors

Shrill forewings of crickets
snake sliding along the earth
leaves hissing in the slight wind
twin skulls of now and then

The human skin
is a distant bell    Listening
to this grey setting
you breathe more wisely
between this space
and that space

# STANFORD STREET POEM

When living
              even with people you love
boils you dry each day
                          what music shall
calm you    Can the sky open *that* wide
to receive your cry


                      The gag of love
steals your tongue    what you know
of soil and sea    flowering and fall

As other bodies call to you
a woman's teeth a man's beard
you approach them    cold leaves in your legs
leaning on an old moonbeam
              the song:
a single crow on the baked bow

                  snow on the Sandias now
                  creamy fields below Taos

                  water in hose will freeze

                  nothing    to reach for

you must
          dance
                    with the trees

# THE MAGDALENA SILVER MINE

Word has reached us here
at the Magdalena silver mine
that you do not love women

"Love" is merely another word
in the American language

But women exist and the word
has gone out that you
don't love them

On my side, I have heard
the Magdalena silver mine exists
but I have never seen it

We could show you photographs

I have photographs of women
(sexually exposed at that)
but I'm not convinced
I have ever seen a woman

What proof do you need?

Only to see a woman

If you saw her
would you love her?

Of course

But if love is, as you said
merely a word...

If I ever saw a woman
I would erase the word "love"
and the Magdalena silver mine
would vanish at the same time

We insist the mine is here
in Magdalena    we have photographs

I have never been in Magdalena

Why don't you simply drive down
from Albuquerque ...

Not without a woman

# KEEPING WATCH

*for* JOY HARJO

"Keep watch over the southwestern sky
until I get there" you write
                              Always
That's what I do to hear myself
during the hours alone with my silence
This particular sky waited a long time
for me
            and now it waits for you

It's a way not a map for my eyes
maybe yours too
                        It's why I've been happier
since I crossed the line near Gallup in '66
The mesas then around 6 o'clock under a hot
September sun were heavy animals
dark brown russet ochre    shaggy and hard
under that constantly moving sky
These calm beasts were friends
whom I recognized as ghosts from a history
I hadn't read except as a child's tale

I watched the sky    this desert ocean
and as I drove I swam in a good sweat
toward a form of home

For you the red horse wind again?
I remember its terrible force once
pulling at your bones
                        It's fearful
to be greeted by your own heart
far from your first cry and bloodspring
as if you'd settled in someone else's dream

I'm still afraid of strangers' myths
but I keep on watching

                         Make it soon
Huge, ancient and flowing as it is
the southwestern sky needs you back
I see it a little paler without you

# JEMEZ STREAM

Wishing you well
the while
the whole day    I
have been there too

Name of that water
on my skin    as it
rolled toward me
from the mesas

Wishing you wonder
in that place    You
and the water
exchanging images

Over stones
the water flows    Sun's quick
flowers mark the course
of the dance

I have been there too
on the margin    illuminated
while time lapsed and
I grew no older

Wishing you joy
and holiness    the whole
day    a golden bird
for your shoulder

so that you leave
for a spell this
century    eyes cooled
in water
                wishing you